SURVIVING THE HOLIDAYS

Survival Guide

GRIEFSHARE®

© MMVII, MMXV by Church Initiative. All rights reserved.
Printed in the United States of America.
Fourth printing of second edition, December MMXIX.

No part of this book may be reproduced or transmitted in any form or by any means—including electronic, mechanical, photocopy, and recording—or by any information storage or retrieval system, without the written permission of the publisher.

For more information:
Church Initiative
P.O. Box 1739
Wake Forest, NC 27588-1739

Phone: 800-395-5755 (US and Canada); 919-562-2112 (local and international)
Fax: 919-562-2114
Email: info@churchinitiative.org
Web address: www.churchinitiative.org, www.griefshare.org

THE HOLY BIBLE, NEW INTERNATIONAL VERSION®, NIV® Copyright © 1973, 1978, 1984, 2011 by Biblica, Inc.® Used by permission. All rights reserved worldwide.

Scripture quotations marked (NLT) are taken from the Holy Bible, New Living Translation, copyright © 1996, 2004, 2007 by Tyndale House Foundation. Used by permission of Tyndale House Publishers, Inc., Carol Stream, Illinois 60188. All rights reserved.

Cover Design by Courtney Navey; Interior Design by Roy Roper, www.wideyedesign.net

WELCOME

The holiday season has begun. This might be the first holiday after your loved one's death, or maybe it's the second, third, or beyond.

In the coming days, you are going to be facing some tough emotions. And due to the nature of Thanksgiving and Christmas—with its focus on family, yearly traditions, expectations, social events, and "cheer"—the emotions can blindside you.

You can lessen the emotional impact by knowing what to expect and being prepared.

Surviving the Holidays is here to help.

Today you will watch a video, be part of a discussion group, and receive a Survival Guide with daily encouragement and helpful exercises for the days ahead.

These tools will enable you not only to survive the coming holidays, but also to face them with a measure of peace and assurance.

In His love,

Steve Grissom

Steve Grissom
GriefShare founder and president
www.griefshare.org

CONTENTS

What to Expect Today viii
Meet the Hosts ix
Meet the Experts ix
About GriefShare xii
Article: A Gift Beyond Comparison xiii

HOLIDAY SURVIVAL GUIDE:
Practical helps for the holiday season 1
Video Note-Taking Outline 3

CHAPTER 1 What to Do with Your Holiday Emotions 7

Survivor Stories 8
The Strength to Survive
- When You'd Rather Skip the Holidays 9
- Emotional Ambushes 10
- Prepare for Hard-Hitting Moments 11
- *Survivor Wisdom:* Where Do You Find the Strength? 12
- You're Never Alone 13
- Are You Numbing Your Pain? 14

Survival Tips
- Help Keep Yourself from Being Blindsided 15
- Write a Grief Letter 16

Holiday Journal 18

CHAPTER 2 Having a Plan................**19**

Survivor Stories................20

The Strength to Survive

- The Importance of Having a Plan................21
- Practical Ideas to Help You Plan................22
- You Can't Duplicate Past Holidays................23
- *Survivor Wisdom:* What New Traditions Could You Try in Honor of Your Loved One?................24
- Laying the Foundation for Your Plan................25
- Help Your Children Survive the Holidays................26
- Take Care of Yourself................28

Survival Tips

- Be Careful Not to Overburden Yourself................29
- Holiday Meals and Baking................31

Holiday Journal................32

CHAPTER 3 Tips for Surviving Social Events................**33**

Survivor Stories................34

The Strength to Survive

- Choosing to Spend Time Alone or with Others................35
- *Survivor Wisdom:* What Kind of People Should You Spend Time with This Holiday?................37
- How to Handle Holiday Invitations................38
- *Survivor Wisdom:* How Do You Respond to Invitations?................39
- *Survivor Wisdom:* How Will You Make It Through That Holiday Event?................40
- "I Don't Want to Bring Others Down"................41

- *Survivor Wisdom:* How Do You Respond to Comments and Questions at the Party?... 42

Survival Tips

- Social Event Survival ... 43
- What to Say When ... 43
- Controlling Negative Self-Talk When You're Alone ... 45

Holiday Journal ... 46

CHAPTER 4 Surviving Thanksgiving and Christmas Day ... 47

Survivor Stories ... 48

The Strength to Survive

- Cherish the Memories ... 49
- Help Others Who Might Need You ... 50
- The Reason for Celebrating the Holidays ... 51
- The Basis for Hope ... 52
- Does It Get Any Easier? ... 53
- Looking Beyond the Holidays ... 54

Survival Tips

- Remembering and Honoring Your Loved One ... 55
- Your Loved One's Legacy ... 56
- Be Thankful ... 57
- Helping Others Helps You ... 58

Holiday Journal ... 60

If You Feel Suicidal ... 62

GriefShare Resources ... 63

WHAT TO EXPECT TODAY

You may be uncertain of what to expect today and a bit apprehensive about being here. Please understand these feelings are normal. By the time this seminar ends, we believe you will be glad you came!

Surviving the Holidays consists of three important components. All three can help you heal and prepare you to face the coming holiday season.

VIDEO

Today you'll watch a video where you'll meet counselors, pastors, and "real-life" people who have experienced the death of a loved one. These people share honestly about:

- Being prepared for surprising emotions that may hit over the holidays
- What to do about traditions and other coming changes
- How to handle holiday parties and invitations
- How to survive potentially awkward moments with other people
- Where to find comfort, strength, and hope in a seemingly hopeless time

Use the note-taking section in this Survival Guide to jot down comments and questions while viewing the video.

DISCUSSION

After the video, you'll have the chance to talk with others who have lost a loved one, discuss what you've learned on the video, and ask questions about any concerns you have. Please understand you do not have to share during the discussion time, but you will still benefit from listening to others.

PERSONAL REFLECTION

Your Survival Guide has practical strategies, words of strength and encouragement, valuable tips, and charts and exercises for daily survival through the holiday season. Take this book home and commit to reading one or two pages per day between now and Christmas. You might choose to read them in the order they are written, or you may skip around and choose your own order.

Also visit **www.griefshare.org/holidays**, where you'll find helpful articles and video clips on holiday survival after the death of a loved one.

> Surviving the Holidays is a special holiday program produced by GriefShare, a grief support group program. We encourage you to find and attend a GriefShare group (**www.griefshare.org**); you will be glad you did.

MEET THE HOSTS

DAVID AND NANCY GUTHRIE are cohosts of the Surviving the Holidays video, and they also host the GriefShare videos. David and Nancy have faced the deaths of two of their three children and now minister to others in grief. They share what they've learned through the Respite Retreats they hold for couples who have lost children, through speaking around the country, and through their books, including *When Your Family's Lost a Loved One*. Nancy has authored several books, including *Holding On to Hope*, *The One Year Book of Hope*, and *Hearing Jesus Speak into Your Sorrow*. David, Nancy, and their son, Matt, live in Nashville, Tennessee.

MEET THE EXPERTS

These experts are featured in the Surviving the Holidays video and Survival Guide.

Sabrina D. Black, author and speaker, is the CEO and clinical director of Abundant Life Counseling Center. She is a limited licensed professional counselor, certified addictions counselor, and certified biblical counselor. She experienced the death of multiple close relatives and the miscarriage of her baby. www.abundantlifecounseling.webs.com

Dave Branon is an editor, a contributor to *Our Daily Bread*, and the author of many devotional articles and books. His book *Beyond the Valley* details his journey after the death of his seventeen-year-old daughter Melissa.

Zoricelis Davila is a bilingual counselor and speaker. She has authored several Spanish books, including ¡*No sé lo que me pasa!* [*I Don't Know What Is Wrong with Me!*]. Her dad died of cancer.

SURVIVING THE HOLIDAYS GRIEFSHARE

ix

Dr. Robert DeVries is professor emeritus of church education at Calvin Theological Seminary. His first wife of twenty-eight years died of cancer. Now remarried to Dr. Susan Zonnebelt-Smeenge, they work together to help people in grief and are coauthors of many books, including *The Empty Chair: Handling Grief on Holidays and Special Occasions* and *From We to Me*.

Dr. Alfonza Fullwood is the senior pastor of Riley Hill Baptist Church in Wendell, North Carolina, and adjunct professor of Preaching and Speech at Southeastern Baptist Theological Seminary. He has led preaching clinics and seminars in North Carolina and abroad and has been in ministry for over three decades.

Omar King is a counselor at Bridgehaven Counseling in Raleigh, North Carolina. He holds a Master's of Divinity with Biblical Counseling degree from Southeastern Baptist Theological Seminary. His mother passed away.

Susan Lutz served as a counselor at the Christian Counseling and Educational Foundation in Glenside, Pennsylvania, for over fifteen years. She now counsels at her church, New Life Presbyterian Church of Dresher. She authored the booklet *Thankfulness: Even When It Hurts*. Her parents passed away.

David Bueno Martin is a bilingual counselor and supervisor at Martin Counseling in Katy, Texas. He also speaks at workshops and seminars. David experienced the loss of a child.
www.martincounseling.com

Dr. Ramon Presson is a certified marriage and family therapist and the founder of LifeChange Counseling and the Marriage Center of Franklin, Tennessee. He has written several books, including *When Will My Life Not Suck?*
www.ramonpresson.com

Lois Rabey is a speaker and writer. She has authored several books, including *When Your Soul Aches* and *Moments for Those Who Have Lost a Loved One*. Lois lost her husband in a hot-air balloon ride accident.

Dr. Paul David Tripp is a pastor, author, and international conference speaker. He is the president of Paul Tripp Ministries and has authored many books, including *Forever* and *A Shelter in the Time of Storm*. Dr. Tripp experienced the death of his father. www.paultripp.com

James White is the pastor at Christ Our King Community Church in Raleigh, North Carolina. He currently serves as the executive vice president of organizational relations for the YMCA of the Triangle and as a board member for Carver Bible College. James experienced the loss of his parents.

H. Norman Wright is a grief therapist and certified trauma specialist. He is the author of over seventy books, including *Experiencing Grief* and *Recovering from Losses in Life*. He experienced the death of his wife and son. www.hnormanwright.com

Dr. Susan Zonnebelt-Smeenge is a licensed clinical psychologist. Her first husband died eighteen years after he was diagnosed with a malignant brain tumor. Now remarried to Dr. Robert DeVries, they work together to help people in grief and are coauthors of many books, including *Getting to the Other Side of Grief* and *Traveling through Grief*.

ABOUT GRIEFSHARE

GriefShare is a network of grief support groups for people grieving the death of a family member or friend. After today's holiday seminar, you will find it helpful and encouraging to attend a weekly GriefShare group.

At GriefShare, you don't have to have it all together. The people there truly understand the raw emotions and daily struggles. They "get it" and won't try to rush you or judge you.

GriefShare is a safe place where you can express your emotions, or where you can choose to just sit quietly and process what you're learning.

At GriefShare you'll discover:

- How to handle the overwhelming emotions
- Where to find the strength to go on
- What to expect in the days to come
- How to grieve in a way that's healthy and suited to you
- What the Bible says about death, grief, and heaven

A GriefShare group includes a weekly video seminar, discussion group, and take-home book. The videos feature respected counselors and teachers who have faced their own grief and "real-life" people who share their struggles and what has helped them. After viewing the video with your group, you'll spend time as a small group discussing the concepts on the video and how they apply to your day-to-day life.

People who have faced the death of a loved one before you can assure you there IS real help. You'll face tough, debilitating emotions in grief and that is completely normal. You are grieving deeply because you loved deeply. But you will make it through, and you can find comfort, healing, and hope again, even amid the grief, pain, and tears.

Taking the step of walking into a GriefShare session is hard, but it may be one of the best decisions you'll make as you seek to survive and then heal from your grief.

GriefShare groups are found in thousands of locations across the nation, Canada, and several other countries. To find a group near you, go to **www.griefshare.org**. You can enter your postal code or city for a list of GriefShare groups meeting nearby. Or you can call the GriefShare offices at 800-395-5755 for help in finding a group near you.

www.griefshare.org, 800-395-5755

A GIFT BEYOND COMPARISON

Sweaters ... gift cards ... a new cell phone? The only gift I want this Christmas is to have my loved one back.

I don't want to decorate and I don't want to party. I want this pain to stop. I want people to quit inviting me over. And I want the holiday season to end.

I'm alone, sad, and angry. I want justice. And the only One able to do anything about it ... isn't.

The weight of your grief can be oppressive at times, especially with the added stress of Thanksgiving and Christmas. You may long for God to do something to ease your pain or to free you from it.

WHAT IS GOD DOING?

In the fog and pain of grief, it can be easy to conclude that God doesn't care about you or that He's unable to help you. But despite how you feel, God has already set a plan in motion to solve your greatest problem. And when you grasp the sacrifice God made to help you, it will be easier to believe that someday He will put an end to your suffering and bring you eternal joy. So how do you get to the point where you can believe that? It starts by considering why Jesus came into the world.

WHY DID JESUS COME?

Jesus came into the world to provide the best gift you could ever receive—the free gift of forgiveness.

"Forgiveness?" you might ask, "Why would I consider that the best gift ever?" The Bible says all of us desperately need God's grace and forgiveness: our actions, thoughts, and motives often fall short of what God requires. And that creates a problem.

So while God, the source of every good and perfect gift, wants to bring you hope, comfort, and peace as you grieve, He also wants you to avoid the consequences of your sin. The Bible says, *"For the wages [payment] of sin is death"* (Romans 6:23a). This verse is talking about spiritual death, which means eternal separation from God, eternal suffering. And God has provided a way to rescue you from that!

You're probably thinking, "I'm hurting enough right

> "But the gift of God is eternal life in Christ Jesus our Lord."
> *Romans 6:23b*

> "For he [God] has rescued us from the kingdom of darkness and transferred us into the Kingdom of his dear Son, who purchased our freedom and forgave our sins."
>
> *Colossians 1:13–14 NLT*

now as it is, and you want to talk about my sin?" If you're asking that question, you're probably just as confused as the people who first learned about who Jesus was and why He came. They were oppressed by their king, Herod, who, according to historians, had many of these Jewish people killed.

No doubt, the people were angered and devastated by their loved one's murders and executions. The Jews longed for a savior who would deliver justice and free them from oppression.

And after the death of your loved one, you may want God to do something similar for you—deliver justice, remove your pain, and free you from your difficult circumstances. But God still wanted those desperately hurting people to know that Jesus came to rescue them from their sins. In fact, God told Joseph to name his son Jesus precisely because *"He will save his people from their sin"* (Matthew 1:21b).

Jesus came into the world to suffer and die so that every person who believes in Him—everyone who has accepted His gift of forgiveness—would escape eternal suffering. Knowing that your sin is forgiven is a source of comfort and hope. That's why it's good to think about it during the holiday season.

WHAT DO I NEED FORGIVENESS FOR?

In the midst of your grief your sin is, understandably, the last thing on your mind. But during the Christmas season it's good to be reminded that we all fall short of God's standard of perfection: by being selfish or rude, lying, being proud, judging, laying blame, having impure thoughts, not being as loving as we could be, etc. So while you may be more morally upright than some people you know, compared to God you're a mess and in desperate need of forgiveness.

RECEIVING THE GIFT

Now, if a friend calls you and tells you that you have a gift waiting at the store, it's not yours until you receive it.

You need to make sure you've received this wonderful gift of forgiveness of sin and an eternity with God. You do that by faith, by simply believing you have disobeyed God and acknowledging your need for Christ to die on the cross in your place—lest you suffer and die for your own sins. Since Jesus is perfect, sin-free, He was able to pay the cost of your sins by His death.

"If we confess our sins, he is faithful and just and will forgive us our sins and purify us from all unrighteousness." (1 John 1:9)

"Now repent of your sins and turn to God, so that your sins may be wiped away. Then times of refreshment will come from the presence of the Lord." (Acts 3:19–20a)

If you would like to receive the gift of forgiveness and acknowledge Jesus' right to lead you, tell God something like this:

> Dear God, I don't always get everything right. In fact, I often stubbornly live life on my own terms, and I now see how wrong that is. Thank you for sending Jesus to suffer and die in my place, for my sins. I'm so glad that Christ lived a perfect life for me and that You accept me as if I've never done anything wrong. You love me very much and want to comfort me, be with me, and uphold me every step of the way. Please lead me and guide me. You're in charge. Show me what I should do in every area of my life. Thank you for forgiving me and granting me an eternity with You. Please help and comfort me as I deal with the pain of grief. Amen.

"Yet God freely and graciously declares that we are righteous. He did this through Christ Jesus when he freed us from the penalty for our sins." (Romans 3:24 NLT)

> "So if the Son sets you free, you will be free indeed."
> — John 8:36

> "The hope of the gospel [what Jesus did for us] is how I get through every day. To honor my daughter's memory and to honor the gift of Jesus, it's my goal to be courageous, to rely on my faith, and to trust God that it'll be okay. And praise the Lord I'll see her again."
>
> – Jeff

WHAT DOES THIS HAVE TO DO WITH MY SUFFERING?

God has given us a wonderful gift that deals with sin, but He also wants to put an end to suffering. He wants to rid the world of tears. And when we realize what He was willing to sacrifice in order to save us from our sin, and remind ourselves that no one can thwart His will, we have no doubt that God can and will remove our pain.

"Since he did not spare even his own Son but gave him up for us all, won't he also give us everything else?" (Romans 8:32 NLT)

God says in the Bible that one day He will completely do away with suffering. There will be no more tears, death, dying, or pain. This is a reality for those who have accepted Christ into their lives.

"He will wipe every tear from their eyes. There will be no more death or mourning or crying or pain, for the old order of things has passed away." (Revelation 21:4)

At Christmas, we celebrate the gift of forgiveness and eternal life that Jesus brought us. His birth marks a new chapter in God's plan to save us from our sin and ultimately end our suffering. So if you're discouraged during the holidays, remind yourself that the baby Jesus came, not only to save you from your sin, but to heal your heart, and the pain of this world. Because of Him, one day there will be no more suffering. And even right now, in the middle of your hurt and suffering, Jesus wants to be a part of your life, to comfort you and help you heal.

GriefShare

HOLIDAY SURVIVAL GUIDE:

PRACTICAL HELPS FOR THE HOLIDAY SEASON

In this section of the book you'll find practical tips, words of strength and encouragement, and charts and exercises to help you face and survive the unique stresses of the holiday season. Take this book home and commit to reading one or two pages per day between now and Christmas. You might choose to read them in the order they are written, or you may skip around and choose your own order. Use the video note-taking outline to take notes while viewing the video seminar.

VIDEO NOTE-TAKING OUTLINE

Use this outline to take notes while viewing the video seminar.

WHY ARE THE HOLIDAYS SO DIFFICULT?

Bittersweet memories

HOW TO APPROACH THE HOLIDAYS

Pain is unavoidable

Don't fake it

Don't numb your pain

THE TEMPTATION TO NUMB PAIN

Suicidal thoughts

PLANNING THE HOLIDAY SEASON

The benefits

How to do it

Know what to expect

Create new traditions

Take it slow

Dealing with guilt

Hold your plans loosely

Talk about your loved one
___
___

HOLIDAY GATHERINGS
Responding to invitations
___
___

Responding to questions
___
___

Responding to challenges
___
___

DEALING WITH HOLIDAY PAIN
Healing takes time
___
___

Help others
___
___

Turn to God
___
___

Be thankful
_____
_____
_____

Remember the meaning of Christmas (Matthew 1:21)
_____
_____

WHEN OTHERS DON'T UNDERSTAND, GRIEFSHARE IS THERE TO ENCOURAGE YOU

After the funeral, when the cards and letters have stopped coming, most people around you return to their normal lives. But your grief continues and you feel alone.

At a weekly GriefShare group, you'll find people who understand and who want to help as you rebuild your life.

Learn more at **www.griefshare.org**.

GRIEFSHARE

GRIEFSHARE **SURVIVING THE HOLIDAYS**

CHAPTER 1:

WHAT TO DO WITH YOUR HOLIDAY EMOTIONS

You open the box of ornaments and stand frozen. A handmade wreath with your child's picture in it. The engraved "Our first Christmas together" silver star. A mini palm tree from last year's trip to the beach. The memories and emotions flood in. Will you make it to January?

What do you do with these emotions? Where do you find the strength to make it through? In this chapter you'll find out:

- What's normal in holiday grief
- How to prepare for emotional ambushes
- How to communicate with people whose well-meaning questions and advice are draining and hurtful
- Where to find the strength to make it through

SURVIVOR STORIES

Often in grief it seems like no one truly understands what you're going through. In the "Survivor Stories" sections in this book, you'll meet people who share some of their struggles during the holidays.

"The things that were so simple before are hard now. It's hard putting up stockings where it used to be three, and now it's two. It's hard putting up decorations. It's hard going shopping when I don't want to be there. I don't care about the gifts. If I could give up everything and not ever get a gift again to have my mom back, I would." – *Shay*

"There was a game Jody and I would play with each other when a certain song would come on at the holiday times, 'Chestnuts roasting on an open fire …' When the next verse would start, 'Jack Frost nipping at your nose,' each of us would try to get to the other person's nose first to nip it. And we'd end up in little tussles with each other; it was a very, very sweet thing that we enjoyed. After Jody died when that song would come on, I couldn't stand to listen to it." – *JoAnne*

THE STRENGTH TO SURVIVE

These short daily readings will help you know what to expect over the holidays and offer encouragement and support in the face of added stress and emotions.

WHEN YOU'D RATHER SKIP THE HOLIDAYS

"I used to feel like I'd like to go to sleep the day before Thanksgiving and wake up January 2nd," admits Lois Rabey.

It's hard enough to get up and make it through a day when you've lost a loved one. But when the expectations of Thanksgiving and Christmas are added on top of that, feelings of loneliness, anxiety, and depression can be compounded.

"As much as we would like to make it go away, that doesn't help," says H. Norman Wright. "What's better is to say, 'This is difficult. But I know I'm going to get through because I'm not dealing with it by myself. I have the Lord, and I'm going to look to Him. As hard as it is, I'm going to take a couple of steps and make this be different.'"

Important steps:

- Recognize that the holidays are going to be tough—emotionally, relationally, physically, spiritually.
- Don't fight the added emotions: accept them and let them come.
- Set realistic expectations for yourself, understanding your limitations.
- Pray and ask God to help you.

"But you, God, see the trouble of the afflicted; you consider their grief and take it in hand. The victims commit themselves to you; you are the helper of the fatherless." (Psalm 10:14)

God, I wish it were January. But I know that pushing aside the pain only makes my grief process longer and harder. I need to face my emotions in order to get through them. I can't do this alone. Thank you that You have all the strength I need and more. Please show me other people, too, who will come alongside me and provide support.

TAKEAWAY:
Experiencing tough emotions over the holidays is normal; don't fight them when they come. Be intentional about prayer.

EMOTIONAL AMBUSHES

You pull out the Christmas ornaments, and you hold in your hand the one with your loved one's name on it.

You go to sign the Christmas cards when suddenly it hits you—*how do I sign this?*

You set the table for the holiday dinner, and without even realizing it, you set a place for your loved one. The emotions pour in like a flood.

"The level of pain will take you by surprise, and you think, How was I not prepared for that? But there are some things you can't be prepared for. And when you get there, recognize, 'That's a normal part of the process. The next time it comes around, it won't be so surprising,'" says Lois Rabey.

H. Norman Wright offers advice: "Tears come at some of the most inopportune times. I think the way we look at tears is important. Tears are one of God's gifts because sometimes we don't have the words and the tears just come.

"You could be at a holiday gathering or in a store, and all of a sudden the tears come. Best thing is, let them come, and don't apologize. Take charge of it and say, 'I'm crying because I've experienced a devastating loss.' That's all you have to say. You're all right. You don't need to be fixed."

When the emotions flood in, God offers a place to go where you can find peace and rest. Emotional ambushes can be exhausting.

"Then Jesus said, 'Come to me, all of you who are weary and carry heavy burdens, and I will give you rest … Let me teach you, because I am humble and gentle at heart, and you will find rest for your souls.'" (Matthew 11:28–29 NLT)

God, I'm worn out from my tears, from the constant emotional overload. When I look at the days ahead, I know I can't make it on my own. I am turning to You because I am worn out and my load is too much to bear alone. Please give me the comfort, wisdom, and strength I need.

TAKEAWAY:

Expect emotional ambushes. It won't stop them, but that expectation will help lessen the surprise factor.

PREPARE FOR HARD-HITTING MOMENTS

"You see two sisters giggling over something Christmassy. They're making their secret plans, and you think—*that's not happening anymore*," shares Emmaline, who experienced the death of one of her two daughters.

As you consider upcoming events or traditions, know that some will be harder to handle than others. Take a moment to try and pinpoint which moments will likely hit you harder than others; for instance, a tradition that your loved one particularly enjoyed.

Emmaline shares a moment that took her by surprise: "I pulled down the stockings, and I'm thinking … *What am I going to do with Rebecca's stocking?* You get blindsided with these little things that you never even think about. Wham, they hit you in the face, and it brings everything back to the forefront."

Understand that hard-hitting moments will come. When they do, you can face the moment, lean into those emotions, and walk through the moment. When you've been blindsided emotionally, you will benefit from opening your Bible and echoing the heartfelt prayers in its pages, such as: "Save me, O God, for the waters have come up to my neck … answer me quickly, for I am in trouble." (Psalm 69:1, 17)

The Bible says that God's Word is living and active and always useful. Incorporate Bible verses into your prayers. It is a powerful practice that brings results—in good and bad times: "So do not fear, for I [God] am with you … I will strengthen you and help you; I will uphold you with my righteous right hand." (Isaiah 41:10)

God, may Your promises in Scripture be my prayer in hard-hitting moments: "Lord, you are always with me; you hold me by my right hand … My flesh and my heart may fail, but you are the strength of my heart and my portion forever." (Psalm 73:23, 26)

TAKEAWAY:
- Think in advance which activities and traditions have the potential to be hard-hitting.
- Plan beforehand to ride out the emotions.
- Pray words directly from the Bible. (Consider memorizing verses and/or getting a Bible app.)

REFLECT:
How are the Scriptures in today's reading helpful to you?

SURVIVOR WISDOM
Advice and encouragement from people who know the pain of loss.

QUESTION: Where Do You Find the Strength?

In the Bible
Reading through the Psalms was a tremendous help. – *Sharon*

Psalm 23 really helped me. I tried to pray that and read it again and again. And not just reading it, [but] trying to understand every word that God was telling me through that Psalm. I just held on to His promises. – *Maria*

In God's promises
If I didn't have the hope and the promise of the gift that God gave us through Jesus, I could not deal with the loss that we've experienced. He promised that I would see Him and I would see my daughter [who died], and that's what keeps me going. – *Emmaline*

Through prayer and helping others
I got on my knees and I cried out and asked God, "Please give me strength, because I don't even want to move. I don't want to do anything. I don't care about anything." After I released it [to God] and I asked for His help, I realized I had some strength. So I put clothes on, and I went to somebody who had been helping me, and I helped them around the house, which made me feel better. – *Shay*

In His people
God and the strength the church brought to me was my rock. – *Eddie*

Church gives me strength. It is positive; it's encouraging. – *Shay*

The memory of my mom as an encourager is what gives me strength. The strength and character in her allowed me to see how to deal with adversity. She trusted God to get her through whatever came her way. – *Gracie*

In thankfulness
I decided I was going to walk around the lake, and I was going to name everything that I was grateful for. So I started walking, and I thanked God for everything: my health, my strength, my right mind, that I can see, that I'm able to walk, the air, the scenery, the trees. The more I said, "Thank you," the taller I was standing. I felt like I had strength with each step. – *Shay*

God is my strength
One of the verses that helped me so much was Psalm 73:26: "My mind and my body may grow weak, but God is my strength; he is all I ever need." – *H. Norman Wright*

So many people told me, "Be strong." What I learned is that it's okay to allow yourself to be weak, to allow yourself to be broken, and to ask God to be your strength. And He will. – *Marne*

YOU'RE NEVER ALONE

The holidays heighten feelings of loneliness. These steps are important in dealing with the pain of being alone:

1. Recognize that loneliness is what you're feeling.
2. Accept the reality of your situation.
3. Discover ways to help ease the lonely times.

"The overwhelming feeling I had my first holiday season was feeling very much alone," shares Mardie. "I didn't feel I was connected to anything or anybody."

While feelings of loneliness may seem overpowering at times during the holidays, you are never alone: "When you think about the fact that God is an ever-present help in times of trouble, that's a perfect time to just fall on your knees and cry out to the Lord and to experience the fact that He is Immanuel, 'God with you,'" says Sabrina Black.

Have you cried out to God, telling Him everything that burdens you and threatens to engulf you? He is the all-sufficient God who loves you intensely, and He wants to show you the healing power of His presence.

"God is our refuge and strength, an ever-present help in trouble. Therefore we will not fear, though the earth give way and the mountains fall into the heart of the sea, though its waters roar and foam and the mountains quake with their surging … The LORD Almighty is with us; the God of Jacob is our fortress." (Psalm 46:1–3, 7)

God, You are the only one who truly knows the loneliness I struggle with. It feels like a hollow in my gut that often threatens to consume me. You are the only one who can remedy that. Please fill that emptiness. I want to know for sure that You're always with me and helping me through. Help me to know and to live out this truth.

TAKEAWAY:
Just because you don't feel God's presence, does not mean He's not there.

REFLECT:
When are you loneliest?

How do you relate to today's passage from Psalm 46?

We encourage you to attend a weekly GriefShare group. Commit to visiting at least three times. You'll find help and healing through GriefShare. For a list of groups in your area, go to **www.griefshare.org** or call **800-395-5755**.

ARE YOU NUMBING YOUR PAIN?

If you try to handle your pain by consistently numbing or avoiding it, the hurt will last longer and will be increasingly difficult to heal from.

Check the box of any descriptions that fit you:

- ☐ Working more hours because it helps me avoid feeling the pain.
- ☐ Overactivity, such as church activities, holiday events, volunteer work, etc.
- ☐ Engaging in sexual activity or a new romantic relationship because it feels good to escape the emotional stress and I long for human touch.
- ☐ Spending money on things I don't need because it momentarily feels good.
- ☐ Taking alcohol or drugs to temporarily numb the pain.
- ☐ Any increased behavior or action that I do because it helps me forget about my pain. (Note, the behavior itself might not be a wrong behavior, but the concern is when you are doing it too much in an effort to avoid your pain.)

"Sex, drugs, alcohol, or shopping can just add a layer of isolation to your life because you're not depending on God; you're not depending on others; you're not even building on the good part of your past. All those behaviors keep you in the place where you're most unhappy," explains Susan Lutz.

Sabrina Black offers this advice for healthy grieving: "Sometimes that void is so large, you'll begin to fill it with other things if you don't fill it with God first. When you're feeling lonely, reach out in prayer or reach out for God's Word found in the Bible. Because there's that sense of emptiness right now, you want to make sure you fill it with an overwhelming presence of God."

If you have a void inside, you need to fill it with something. Choose wisely.

"Keep away from anything that might take God's place in your hearts." (1 John 5:21 NLT)

God, this is so hard. I can't do this alone. I can do this with You. Fill me with You— Your comfort and reassurance, Your promises, Your wisdom, and strength.

TAKEAWAY:
Be intentional about filling your void with good, godly things.

SURVIVAL TIPS

The charts, checklists, and exercises in this section will help you apply the practical ideas in this book to your own life.

HELP KEEP YOURSELF FROM BEING BLINDSIDED

Emotional ambushes are triggered by activities, traditions, songs, sights, sounds, etc., that remind you of past times with your loved one. Mentally preparing yourself will help lessen the ambush factor.

"Going into that first holiday season after the death of your loved one, a number of things could catch you off guard. One thing you ought to do is replay in your own mind, well ahead of time, what the family traditions almost always involved so that you are expecting these things to happen.

"So if your aunt [who died] always comes with a banana cream pie, somebody bringing a banana cream pie may trigger some emotion for you. Or if your father always cut the turkey, who's going to do that?" – Dr. Robert DeVries

Answer the questions below to help you think through potentially hard-hitting moments.

HOLIDAY PREPARATIONS

Your loved one likely had a certain role in decorating for the holidays, cooking/baking, gift-giving, etc. How will holiday preparations look different this year?

_____

_____

_____

_____

HOLIDAY GET-TOGETHERS

How has the death affected who you'll be getting together with this holiday, compared to past holidays? (Will you miss seeing certain people; is there potential for awkwardness or discomfort; is there a possibility of conflict; etc.?)

_____

_____

_____

THANKSGIVING/CHRISTMAS DAY

What will you miss most about your loved one's presence on Thanksgiving/Christmas day?

_____

_____

_____

_____

WRITE A GRIEF LETTER

Over the holidays, everyone wants to know how you are doing. Their questions, while well-intentioned, can wear you out, as you repeat the same emotionally draining responses.

Other people are full of advice and want to help you by barging in and trying to take over your healing process: "Do this, eat this, read this, go here, go there."

H. Norman Wright suggests you write a grief letter before the holiday season (or prior to specific events). Send it to family and friends, or carry copies with you to pass out to people as needed.

BASIC STEPS

1. Briefly describe your experience and your feelings.
2. Let people know what they can expect from you.
3. Tell them what they can do and say that you'd find comforting, and share what's not comforting.
4. List specific, practical needs they can help with.

Note: Your emotions will be unique to you. There is no right or wrong way to grieve. In writing your own grief letter, you are welcome to use any ideas in the following samples that best fit you.

SAMPLE HOLIDAY GRIEF LETTERS
SAMPLE 1

> As you know, I'm going into this holiday without my ____. I don't want to ruin the holidays for everyone else, but to be honest, I have no holiday cheer. I won't isolate myself this holiday, but I will probably have to excuse myself early from get-togethers or spend time alone in a different room. I don't feel like talking much.

I'm going to cry. A lot. And probably in the middle of your party. My tears are necessary for my healing and recovery, so don't be embarrassed by them. Pat my shoulder, give me a brief hug, and let me know you are praying for me and that you are there. Words are not necessary.

Please talk about my loved one. It would hurt me so much if you avoid speaking his/her name. I like to hear stories and memories about him/her.

My energy level is going to be low this season. I can't do everything I used to do. If someone is available to help me with some home and holiday tasks, that would be appreciated. Specifically, I need someone to help me put up and take down a small tree. I could stand help with some housework too (I can't seem to keep up with it). While I would appreciate help with some specific tasks, please don't try to take over my healing or offer advice.

Thank you for caring about me and praying for me. Your love and concern is a comfort.

SAMPLE 2

As you know, I'm going into this holiday without my _____. I would like to get out and be around people, but I'm not ready to talk about my emotions. Let me know you care by offering a listening ear and a shoulder, but do not press me to talk beyond that.

I might not be the best company, but I would appreciate it if you'd help get me out of the house a little more this holiday season. I would enjoy having someone to attend the [annual holiday concert, children's Christmas play, holiday open house tour, etc.] with. I don't want to put up my Christmas tree or bake cookies alone this year, but I'd still like to include those traditions in my home, if anyone would like to join me in that. I would be glad to join you for a meal or celebration; don't hesitate to invite me.

I know you care for me and want to offer words of comfort and advice, but please keep your words few at this point. Thank you for your presence and your prayers. Your love and concern is a comfort.

HOLIDAY JOURNAL:

WHAT TO DO WITH YOUR HOLIDAY EMOTIONS

A journal provides you an opportunity to face and deal with tough situations; it gives you a place to release pent-up emotions. It doesn't have to be neat, nor contain good grammar or spelling. Your journal is there as a healing tool, for your eyes only.

Use a separate notebook or journal to write your responses to one or more of the topics below.

- ☐ Psalm 147:3 says that Jesus heals the brokenhearted and binds up their wounds. Tell Jesus about why your heart is broken this holiday season and ask Him to bind up your wounds.

- ☐ Read the comment below and share your personal thoughts about crying or showing emotions in public.

    "Emotions are natural for all of us, and yes, other people may become uncomfortable with them, but they're genuine emotions. The Bible is filled with examples of people weeping in public. Crying is not shameful at all. A good show of emotion from time to time, even at a party, shows authenticity for the significant loss you've experienced in your life." – Dr. Robert DeVries

- ☐ Make a list of all the emotions you've been struggling with recently. (Optional: It's also very helpful to take each emotion separately and analyze it, by answering questions such as "What is this about? What exactly is triggering this emotion? What is at the heart of this issue?" Don't try to do this all in one sitting.)

CHAPTER 2:

HAVING A PLAN

By taking time to plan—what you'll do and not do this holiday season—you'll have a degree of control over incoming emotions. And when life feels out of control, this is helpful.

This chapter discusses:

- Whether or not to continue holiday traditions that are so hard without your loved one
- Why having a plan is crucial
- How to create a straightforward, yet flexible, plan
- How to take care of yourself and your children this season

SURVIVOR STORIES

Jeannine was surprised to find out she didn't know how to put up the tree she and her husband had always used. And Jeff, after his daughter's death, couldn't decide whether or not to continue a special tradition they'd always done as a family. You will face similar situations and decisions.

"My husband always decorated our tree the day after Thanksgiving. I couldn't put up the tree. I didn't know how to put it together. It was one of those old trees that had all the spokes to it. So one of the pastors came and put my tree up for me, put the lights on, and then helped me decorate it. Then after that, I couldn't take the tree down because I didn't know how to take it apart. So we left it up until the middle of February." – *Jeannine*

"We have a silly tradition at Christmas that we've done since our daughters were little kids. We have Santa Claus hats and reindeer antlers that light up, and in the past we've all put on our Santa Claus hats to go Christmas shopping or to go a party or a church function. I couldn't do that this year. All the hats and the antlers sat right there where I saw them every single day. I just couldn't do it." – *Jeff*

THE STRENGTH TO SURVIVE

These short daily readings will help you decide what to do about your own holiday traditions and will help you create a meaningful, do-able, flexible plan that is suited to you.

THE IMPORTANCE OF HAVING A PLAN

"Winging it is a poor choice if you're dealing with the holidays. Often it comes from, *I don't want to think about it; I don't want to deal with it*. But not thinking about it doesn't mean the holidays are going to disappear," says Dr. Susan Zonnebelt-Smeenge.

As you approach the holidays, you will be faced with events, memories, traditions, expectations, and responsibilities. Having a plan keeps you from becoming overwhelmed. Dr. Robert DeVries shares:

- Planning simply means that you decide what and how much you want to do.
- Prioritizing means that if there are fifteen different activities you might be involved in over the holiday season, which one or two are most important to you?

Whatever you plan, be sure to allow yourself flexibility to adjust it. (And if you have children, involve them in the planning process; this will be significant in their healing as well.) The thought of making a plan can seem daunting. You don't have to make your plan alone. Involve God in the planning process, and listen for His direction. Use the charts and tips in this book to guide you. Ask a family member or friend to help you make your plan.

"Good planning and hard work lead to prosperity, but hasty shortcuts lead to poverty." (Proverbs 21:5)

God, while my first inclination is to say, "I don't want to even think about planning for the holidays," I do want to get well, I do want to be able to face the holidays, and I want to honor my loved one this holiday season. But I need Your help. Help me decide which activities to prioritize and which I can set aside, and grant me the courage and strength to follow through. I will listen for Your guidance.

TAKEAWAY:
Having a plan helps keep you from becoming overwhelmed.

REFLECT:
What concerns do you have about creating a plan?

Look at Dr. DeVries' definition of planning above. How does it help relieve some of your concerns?

PRACTICAL IDEAS TO HELP YOU PLAN

You can't do it all this holiday season. Whatever you think you must do, consider how you could simplify the plans that seem overwhelming or that may be a financial burden. (See the Survival Tips at the end of this chapter to help you put your plan on paper.)

Look for a balance between meaningful and manageable.

Decorating: You don't have to put up every decoration. Consider which decorations are most important this year, in light of your circumstances and energy level (and next year you may choose differently). If you choose to have a tree, you do not need to use all the ornaments you normally would. Have young relatives help you decorate. Decorate your tree with small stuffed animals instead of ornaments. Consider a tabletop tree or a meaningful centerpiece that focuses on the true meaning of Christmas. Use items from nature to decorate.

Shopping: Realize you don't need to purchase a gift for everyone this year. If finances are tight, consider a personal message in a card, a gift of a casserole, or a bag filled with candy for the children. Be up-front with family and friends about changes in gift-giving. Also, to avoid a potentially stressful mall experience, shop online or from catalogs; these gifts can be sent directly to recipients.

Holiday cooking: Consider ways to simplify holiday meals: have each guest bring a dish, lay out a simple buffet with turkey sandwiches and dressing, order dinner from a local grocery store or restaurant, go out, or ask someone else to host this year's meal. You could also skip cookie baking or only make one kind of cookie this year.

"Then you will call, and the LORD will answer; you will cry for help, and he will say: Here am I." (Isaiah 58:9a)

Lord, I need to make changes in my plans this year, but I don't want to let anyone down. Help me make wise decisions regarding holiday preparations. Please give me the courage to speak up and let others know I will be celebrating more simply this year and that I'd appreciate their support and understanding.

TAKEAWAY:
Decide in advance how you can make holiday preparations meaningful, yet manageable.

YOU CAN'T DUPLICATE PAST HOLIDAYS

You might wonder if it's better to try and keep the holidays the same as possible or whether to do something completely different this year. There is no right or wrong answer to this question, as long as you recognize that you cannot duplicate past holidays.

"There may be sadness in the fact that a holiday is never going to be the same after a loss. But I think it's better than adopting a crushing burden of trying to recreate something that cannot be recreated," says Susan Lutz.

You will need to prayerfully consider what is best for you and your family this year, and then next year you might decide to do things differently.

"I was putting too much pressure on myself in my desire to make things as normal as possible for my husband and my father-in-law that first Christmas after my mother-in-law died," says Connie.

JoAnne shares, "It really helped me to get away and do Christmas differently than we'd ever done it before. The first year after Jody died, I took a trip to South Florida with my sons. It helped not to have those strong emotional memories in my face. We did that for the next four years."

"Cast your cares on the Lord and he will sustain you." (Psalm 55:22)

Lord, what would be best for me this holiday season? What plans would be helpful for my healing and still be respectful to my family members? Teach me how to hear Your voice and follow closely after You. You know what's best for me. Thank you for guiding me through Your words in the Bible and through the wise counsel of mature Christian friends.

TAKEAWAY:
Consider in advance how much you'll try to keep things the same this year and what you'll do differently.

REFLECT:

Which holiday traditions/events do you think you'll try to maintain this year?

What do you think of JoAnne's idea to go someplace completely different for Christmas?

How will you put Psalm 55:22 into practice in your holiday decision-making?

SURVIVOR WISDOM

Advice and encouragement from people who know the pain of loss.

QUESTION: What New Traditions Could You Try in Honor of Your Loved One?

Before we open presents, we all share a special Christmas memory or what makes Christmas special to us. – *Connie*

What we've decided to do is to make a "dad tree," and we decorate it with all sorts of ornaments that relate to the university he went to, his favorite football team, and the things he enjoyed doing, like fishing. We put a baseball cap with his school emblem on the top. – *Sheila*

Several years at Christmas we've all walked out to the graveyard, and we take a little Christmas tree. – *Jemma*

My children and I light a candle for my [deceased] husband through the whole month of December every night at dinner. I've made a candle for them with a picture of them and their father wrapped around the candle. – *Sheila*

My husband loved holidays. On Christmas day I made sure I put on something festive. [My children and grandchildren and I] talked about all the things he would say and laugh about, things he would tell the children, and things he would do. – *Carolyn*

I prayed and asked the Lord to help me find a gift for everyone in the family to remember my husband. – *Jeannine*

Give gifts to a cause that meant a lot to your loved one. – *Susan Lutz*

This year on Christmas Eve day, my children and I went to a shelter and helped out. We prepared meals and we prepared toys. – *Christina*

I visited a girlfriend of mine who was single and by herself. – *Lois Rabey*

We have tons of ornaments we've made throughout our lives, and my mom has taken all of Hannah's ornaments and put them in a separate box. The whole family puts Hannah's ornaments on the Christmas tree together. – *Jemma*

My family decided we would come together and have a celebration in honor of my sister-in-law, and we would all open the gifts we had purchased for her. As we opened the gifts, we tried to do an imitation of her and tried to react as she would when she would open the gift. We had such a great time remembering her in a special way. We decided that every year we would buy silly gifts in remembrance of her. – *Sabrina Black*

LAYING THE FOUNDATION FOR YOUR PLAN

As you make decisions about what activities to participate in, who to spend time with, and how to handle unexpected situations, you'll want to lay the right foundation for your plans. Dr. Paul David Tripp describes three considerations:

Know yourself. Know your strengths and weaknesses. Make plans that focus on your strengths, and be cautious about those that might bring out your weaknesses. If spending time with your grandchildren or nieces and nephews brings you joy, plan a visit. If, at the office party, you might be tempted to numb your pain with alcohol—don't go. Put things on the calendar that will refresh your spirit: Lunch with a same-sex Christian friend? An outdoor hike alone with God? A special church worship service or concert?

Know your family and friends. You have an idea of how family and friends will respond to you and what type of advice or support they'll give. Plan to spend time with those who will listen to you, lift you up, and encourage you in your faith. Plan to avoid those who will rush you in your grief or who will encourage you to lower your moral standards.

Know God. Know what God has promised to supply and deliver. "What has God said He will do for me in this particular moment?" Commit to reading and studying your Bible to find out (you can use online Bible study tools, ask your pastor or a Christian friend for guidance, or check if your Bible has a topical index or concordance). Not knowing what God promises sets you up to miss out on the help He offers, or to be disappointed because you're expecting God to do something He never said He'd do.

Building a foundation based on who you are and what God has promised will help ease your pain and keep you standing firm when you're floundering or wishing to escape. You'll also gain a greater awareness of God's faithfulness and provision in your life.

"The LORD is trustworthy in all he promises and faithful in all he does." (Psalm 145:13b)

God, You know me better than anyone, and You have promised to help me in all situations. Please help me to be prepared and strengthened for the coming days. You will never let me down. Thank you.

TAKEAWAY:
When you consider where to go and which people to spend time with, build your plan around who you are and what God has promised you in this situation.

HELP YOUR CHILDREN SURVIVE THE HOLIDAYS

Your children might have concerns about the coming holidays. *How are we going to cut down the Christmas tree without Dad? Who is going to make our special Christmas breakfast? If we aren't going to Grandma's for dinner, where will we go?*

They, too, will struggle with sadness, loneliness, and anger. In your holiday planning, make a point to think about …

1. How you'll prepare your children for the changes this season.
2. How you'll help them communicate and express their emotions.

Talk with them ahead of time: "I talked to my children before the holiday season started. I said, 'We're going to do the best that we can and celebrate what the season's about, even though Daddy's gone. He would want us to do that. We're going to have some new traditions, and it will be okay. This will feel different. There may be things that happen that you're going to feel sad about. Come talk to me, and we'll work through it with God's help,'" shares Lois Rabey.

Include them in holiday planning: Include your children in the planning, says Dr. Robert DeVries. "When my first wife died, we had a very hardy discussion among the three children and myself: yes, we do want the tree; no, we don't have to put all the lights up outdoors; we're going to have our normal Christmas brunch, but we don't have to do Christmas cards."

Help them express their emotions: Your children might be ambushed by emotions this holiday season. And when kids are upset about something, they often don't express their feelings in words. Instead, their fears and anxieties can come out in the form of misbehavior, throwing fits, or unusual quietness and withdrawal. Spend time working alongside or playing with your kids and open the door of communication by sharing what you're feeling (then make sure you listen instead of talk!). Consider introducing healthy emotional outlets such as clay sculpting, coloring, or water play, which can be springboards for sharing.

Ask others for help and keep your family holiday plans simple. Encourage your children to talk to God about their hurts and worries. Let them

> **REFLECT:**
> What will you do to help your children with their emotions and anxieties this holiday season?

know that with Jesus by their side, they can have peace, safety, and hope, even when they feel sad.

"And surely I am with you always, to the very end of the age." (Matthew 28:20b)

Lord, taking care of my children is so difficult when I'm hurting this badly. Please give me a supernatural strength that will enable me to guide my children through healthy grieving. I will entrust my children to You. I pray that they come to have a relationship with You.

REFLECT:

How will you open the lines of communication with your children (or guide them to another safe adult to share with)?

TAKEAWAY:

Your children are grieving too, and they need help in preparing for the changes and emotional burdens of the season.

Attending a weekly GriefShare support group will help you to know what's normal in grief, how to handle the tough emotions, how to take care of yourself, and where to find comfort. To find a GriefShare support group near you, go to **www.griefshare.org** or call **800-395-5755**.

TAKE CARE OF YOURSELF

What have you been doing to take care of yourself this holiday season? Don't forget self-care in your holiday planning this year.

"It isn't healthy to expect yourself to be able to do all the things you used to do. Pacing yourself and having patience with yourself is so important," advises Dr. Susan Zonnebelt-Smeenge.

Emotional/mental health: Be sure that part of your holiday planning includes time for reflection, for processing the new emotions and stresses that come with the holidays. As you face a holiday experience, an emotion, or memory, write down what happened, how you reacted, how you feel about it now, and what you can learn from it. Use the Holiday Journal sections in this book to guide you in writing out your thoughts and emotions.

Physical health: The holidays will be easier to face if you get enough rest, get some exercise and sunlight, and make wise food choices. "For me," shares Connie, "not getting enough rest made me vulnerable to not just being a weary griever, but also a depressed believer."

Spiritual health: Spiritual renewal and focus is a must. Only God can truly heal the pain of loss. "Open your Bible and meditate on the Word of God," says Sabrina Black. "The Twenty-third Psalm says, 'The Lord is.' Stop there and meditate on all the things the Lord is. Especially during your time of pain, the Lord is your comfort; the Lord is your lover; the Lord is your keeper; the Lord is your safe place; the Lord is your refuge."

"He leads me beside quiet waters, he refreshes my soul. He guides me along the right paths." (Psalm 23:2b–3a)

Lord God, sometimes I don't do a very good job of taking care of myself. I know what to do, but then I don't do it. Please strengthen me to make wise decisions about my body, my time, my emotional responses, and my spiritual focus. With You, I can do all things, and I can walk forward each day under Your protection.

TAKEAWAY:
Be intentional about self-care.

REFLECT:
In what ways this holiday season do you think you'll try to please other people (or do what they expect), possibly at your own expense?

What action will you take to benefit your health?

SURVIVAL TIPS

The charts, checklists, and exercises in this section will help you apply the practical ideas in this book to your own life.

BE CAREFUL NOT TO OVERBURDEN YOURSELF

"Think about what would make the holidays manageable and meaningful."
– Dr. Ramon Presson

Your energy is likely low this holiday season. It's wise to plan ahead and set careful limits on what you're able to do this year. But be flexible. What you decide today might change later, and that's okay.

HOLIDAY DECORATIONS

1. Check the items below you'd like to do, those most important to you.
2. Describe how you might do them in a way that won't overburden you (see examples.)

☐ Tree (e.g., get a smaller tree, buy a pre-decorated tree, have your grandchildren decorate and take down the tree you've always used, enlist help from a friend)

_____
_____
_____
_____

☐ Interior/exterior lights (e.g., only put lights inside this year, ask for help putting out exterior lights, use small electric candles in the windows instead)

_____
_____
_____
_____

☐ Other decorations

_____
_____
_____
_____

HAVING A PLAN GRIEFSHARE

CHRISTMAS CARDS

Check what you might do this year. Only send cards if it is important/meaningful to you.

- ☐ Skip cards.
- ☐ Send a card or note via email or social media.
- ☐ Limit the number of cards you send (e.g., only to out-of-town relatives).
- ☐ Send a photo card of a beautiful scene, Scripture, or preprinted meaningful message. Or send a current family photo where you are holding in your arms a picture of your deceased loved one.
- ☐ Ask someone to help you with cards: _____

GIFT-GIVING

Check ideas that will help keep gift-giving at a manageable level.

- ☐ Buy gift cards.
- ☐ Shop online or by catalog. Ask someone to help, if needed: _____
- ☐ Shop early.
- ☐ Ask someone to go shopping with you, someone who will understand that this might be overwhelming for you: _____
- ☐ Brainstorm low-cost gift ideas, such as bags of assorted treats or framed photos.
- ☐ Consider passing on something special that belonged to your loved one.
- ☐ Give a gift to a cause important to your loved one in lieu of presents.
- ☐ Choose not to give gifts to everyone on your list, and prayerfully consider how to communicate that to family members.

HOLIDAY MEALS AND BAKING

Perhaps in the past you've done the bulk of the holiday meals and baking—and you truly enjoyed it. Or maybe your deceased loved one was the person who spearheaded the holiday cooking.

You'll want to be cautious this year about not overburdening yourself, or others, in an attempt to keep things as close to "normal" as possible.

"Our Christmas tradition was that my husband [now deceased] would get up and cook breakfast. That first Christmas I bought donuts the night before because I knew I wouldn't be able to cook breakfast." – Jeannine

Check ideas that might work for you this year.

- ☐ Allow someone else to host the Thanksgiving or Christmas meal.
- ☐ Have a potluck supper, where no one is responsible for the bulk of the cooking.
- ☐ Go out to a restaurant.
- ☐ Pre-order a turkey/ham and side dishes.
- ☐ Choose not to make everything from scratch that you typically do.
- ☐ Enlist cleaning help for both before and after meals. Excuse yourself from this, if needed.
- ☐ Instead of inviting people for a large meal, have people for desserts and coffee instead.
- ☐ Buy cookies or desserts from the store or use ready-bake cookies.
- ☐ Participate in a cookie exchange (where a group of friends each make four dozen of one type of cookie, and then everyone shares to create a variety platter to bring home).
- ☐ Other ideas: _____
  _____

ASK FOR AND ACCEPT HELP

Your family and friends may be looking for ways to come alongside you and lessen your pain. Allow them to support you in concrete ways. Let them do or help with the thing you would like to see done, yet have no energy to do. Regarding holiday meal responsibilities that you usually take care of, ask yourself, Is this something someone else can do? Or is this something someone might enjoy helping me with?

HOLIDAY JOURNAL:
HAVING A PLAN

"We have a tendency to think of prayer as talking to God, a monologue. But if prayer is really a dialogue, after we express ourselves to God, we listen for what He might want to say to us. And I encourage people to do that by journaling."
– Dr. Ramon Presson

Be sure that part of your holiday planning includes time for reflection, for processing and talking with God about the emotions and stresses of the holidays. Use a separate notebook or journal to reflect on the topics below. Let this be a healing tool.

- ☐ The sights, sounds, and smells of the holiday season will trigger new waves of emotions and memories: Christmas lights in the neighborhood. Carols on the radio. Apple pie in the oven. Write about the sights, sounds, and smells that have been an emotional trigger for you. How did you react?

    Holiday sights
    _____

    Sounds
    _____

    Smells
    _____

- ☐ Lois Rabey, whose husband died, says to "Lean into the reality that God loves you." Describe how you've been leaning in to God and your struggles to do so. Write this in the form of a letter to God.

CHAPTER 3:

TIPS FOR SURVIVING SOCIAL EVENTS

"You have to come for the party! It will be good for you, plus you don't want to let anyone down." So you go to the party with a plastic smile, cringe at people's "well-meaning" comments, hide out in the bathroom, and escape the party as soon as possible. Family get-togethers, office parties, yearly social events—all can be difficult for the person in grief.

This chapter offers practical ideas on:

- Whether to attend the holiday event
- How to communicate your decision with the host
- How to handle awkward moments
- What to say to people who make hurtful comments
- What to do in the face of tears and emotional overload

SURVIVOR STORIES

Sheila and Gerri faced opposite situations at a social event. In Sheila's case, family and friends didn't talk enough, and for Gerri, her friend's words hurt to the core.

"It was the first Christmas after my husband passed. My family does a reunion, and I was worried about going. I thought people were going to say, 'How are you doing?' 'What's it like?' And there was none of that—*there was no mention of my husband's name*. The emotions that I felt going to that reunion without him, and then getting there and thinking, 'Wow. Nobody really cares anymore. Everybody's gone on with their life. It's six months later.' On the inside I was very broken."
– *Sheila*

"After my husband died, during the first holidays one of my friends said to me, 'Well, you know that's his family and they may not have room for you anymore.' I thought, 'Where did that come from?' And why would she choose the most vulnerable time in my life to share that with me? It was unbearable." – *Gerri*

THE STRENGTH TO SURVIVE

These short daily readings will help you to find a healthy balance between time spent alone and time spent with others, and to discover how both can be helpful. You'll also find practical suggestions on how to survive social events.

CHOOSING TO SPEND TIME ALONE OR WITH OTHERS

You might prefer surrounding yourself with people during the holidays, which helps you forget your pain, or maybe you'd rather shut your doors and turn out your lights, avoiding people altogether. To heal from your pain, you need a healthy balance of privacy and interaction; and to experience the benefits of each, it's important to evaluate situations before you are in them. Here are a few questions to ask yourself before committing to a planned time of privacy or interaction.

If I choose to be with people today, will I:

- Talk about my loved one and share memories about him or her?
- Safely express my grief if I am ambushed by difficult emotions?
- Be honest and ask for any needed help?

If I choose to be alone, will I take the time to:

- Digest my latest feelings and thoughts?
- Talk to God about those feelings, seek His help, and accept His comfort?
- Avoid the temptation to numb my pain (drink excessively, take drugs, look at pornography, overeat, etc.)?

If you would answer no to any of the above questions, rethink going into the situation, or take steps to make the experience more beneficial. For instance, if you realize you might not be able to talk about your loved one at a family gathering, write a grief letter to give to those who will be there.* If you realize that, when alone, all you're going to do is focus on your sadness and despair, plan to read a book on healing from grief instead.

> **REFLECT:**
>
> Name someone in your life who fits the description in the first three bullets in this article.
>
> When you choose to be alone, what do you tend to do?

TIPS FOR SURVIVING SOCIAL EVENTS

REFLECT:

What suggestions in this article will you apply to help your healing process?

"[Jesus] went up on a mountainside by himself to pray ... He was there alone." (Matthew 14:23b)

"Two are better than one ... If either of them falls down, one can help the other up." (Ecclesiastes 4:9–10a)

God, even though my thoughts are scattered, give me the ability to think ahead about the situations I'm going to be in. Help me know what steps to take to allow both time with others and time alone to contribute to my healing.

TAKEAWAY:

Find a healthy balance of time spent alone and with others. Be intentional about making those times healthy.

* See page 16 for instructions on writing a grief letter.

WEEKLY ENCOURAGEMENT AS YOU REBUILD YOUR LIFE

GriefShare is a friendly, caring group of people who will walk alongside you through one of life's most difficult experiences. You don't have to go through the grieving process alone.

Learn more at **www.griefshare.org**.

GRIEF**SHARE**®

SURVIVOR WISDOM

Advice and encouragement from people who know the pain of loss.

QUESTION: What Kind of People Should You Spend Time with This Holiday?

It's important to identify who are the safe people in your life. Who are the ones who are going to nurture you, to build you up? Not to berate you or say, "Well, get over it. You know it's been six months now." – *H. Norman Wright*

Try hard not to get in that circle of friends who lean toward vices you know are going to be detrimental to your recovery. – *Dr. Alfonza Fullwood*

You want somebody who's not afraid of suffering, somebody who knows you'll get through on the other side and who is ready to walk with you and wait with you as that process continues. – *Susan Lutz*

Church can be one of the places that's the most difficult to go to, but church is also the place you're going to receive the most help and care. – *Lois Rabey*

When I've had such desperate feelings of loneliness, especially at the holidays, it's been important for me to see how other folks have felt the same way and to be told, "Hang on; it feels like you might not make it, but you are going to make it." – *JoAnne*

There are places that only you and the Lord can go in your grief, and you need somebody who recognizes that. You want somebody who knows that ultimately your healing is not going to come from within yourself. Your healing is going to come when you learn to bring all your pain and loss to the Lord. That person will kindly but persistently encourage you in that direction. – *Susan Lutz*

It was hard to make it through with no family around, so I made some phone calls and tried to get closer to the people at church; I felt like they were part of my family. – *Bill*

HOW TO HANDLE HOLIDAY INVITATIONS

Other people do not know what to expect from you during the holidays. Should they invite you to their party? Should they insist you come? Should they leave you alone?

Not only do others not know what's best for you, you're not sure yourself! You're probably torn between desiring to please your family and friends—and being uncertain if you can even make it through a social event without an emotional breakdown.

These practical suggestions will help lower the stress of facing invitations and events:

- **Decide in advance to attend some events, but to say no to others.** Communicate this to people up front. Give them time to process and accept that you're doing things differently this year.

- **Only plan to stay a portion of the time.** Tell your host of this possibility beforehand.

- **Learn to say no.** When someone insists it would be "good for you" to attend, explain that right now you're not capable of handling as many functions as before. H. Norman Wright says, "Instead of trying to meet the expectations of others, it's best to say, 'Thanks for offering that advice [or invitation], but here's what I've decided to do ...' When they pressure you, repeat word for word what you've already said."

- **Never feel guilty about not going at the last minute.** When accepting an invitation, let the host know that if you don't feel up to it on the day of the event, you might back out at the last minute. See if that's okay with the host. And if you're having a tough time on the day of the event, Sabrina Black suggests, "Let your host know you're not able to make it. Thank your host for the invitation, and encourage him or her to invite you again. You need to do what's best for you in this hour."

"Cast all your anxiety on him because he cares for you." (1 Peter 5:7)

REFLECT:
What concerns do you have about holiday events or get-togethers?

God, worrying about how to respond to holiday invitations can be such a burden. Please give me the courage to attend events, and the courage to decline invitations or back out if I need to. Help me to not be so concerned about what others will think as I process whether to attend or not. Thank you for being here for me.

TAKEAWAY:
Follow these ideas to help lower the stress of making decisions about holiday events.

SURVIVOR WISDOM

Advice and encouragement from people who know the pain of loss.

QUESTION: How Do You Respond to Invitations?

You might say, "Can you just hold my invitation lightly? I'm planning on coming, but it may change that day." – *H. Norman Wright*

Don't commit to that party just because you want to please someone. Just be honest and say, "I'm still in the process, some good days, some not so good, so I'll let you know." – *Zoricelis Davila*

I would pick and choose to be involved with some things that friends were doing, but not a lot. – *JoAnne*

You don't have to do it all. Picking one or two holiday events and trying to make yourself get through those is all you need to do. You can take that responsibility and make it through. – *Dr. Susan Zonnebelt-Smeenge*

Sometimes it helps to find out, who else is going to be at this gathering? Are these people you feel comfortable with, that you want to spend some time with? – *H. Norman Wright*

You might have to learn to be assertive because you might say to people:
"I can only come for an hour."
"Oh no, no, you need to come for the whole time."
"Thank you for the invite, but I will be able to come for an hour."
And you repeat that two or three times in a very gentle, loving way.
– *H. Norman Wright*

I challenge people not to do the "all or nothing." What is healthy for each of us is to try to do "something." I'd say, "I'm going to go with the goal, first, of just staying a half an hour. And if I make it, I can leave."
– *Dr. Susan Zonnebelt-Smeenge*

Plan a different time to get together

I found that making the holiday visit either just before the holiday or after the holiday made for a much better visit. I didn't have to fight the holiday traffic. I was able to have quality time with the people that I wanted to visit. I was able to actually have a conversation without all the noise in the background, and it worked much better. – *Mardie*

SURVIVOR WISDOM

Advice and encouragement from people who know the pain of loss.

QUESTION: How Will You Make It Through That Holiday Event?

I always drove myself so I could leave whenever I wanted to.
– *Dr. Susan Zonnebelt-Smeenge*

Sometimes it feels scary to think about walking into someplace by yourself. What worked for me was to set a meeting place right outside of the door of wherever we were going, and [plan to] go with somebody.
– *Dr. Susan Zonnebelt-Smeenge*

There were times at the parties that I just needed to get away, cry until I was done, and then I could go back. I found that really helpful. – *Carla*

One day when visiting family, I didn't want to be around people, and I excused myself to a back room. I chose to take care of myself instead of worrying about making other people comfortable. – *Charlaine*

When I went to an event, I found a way to let people know I wanted to talk about my husband and I wanted to hear their stories.
– *Dr. Susan Zonnebelt-Smeenge*

What you can say is, "I really wish so and so were here today. This was one of their favorite holidays." Confronting the feelings honestly and not avoiding them gives you a great chance to reminisce and to really talk about the influence that person had. – *Julie*

It may be at that party you can be laughing at eight o'clock and crying at eight-thirty because something triggered it. Don't be embarrassed about laughing, because even in the midst of our sorrow there's joy. It's all mixed up together, and it doesn't come in sequence. – *Dr. Robert DeVries*

Sometimes I find myself not wanting to be fully in the moment because the pain is there. When I find myself upstairs in my room, and all the noise downstairs, I've got to say, "I am too far away from the activities of this holiday; let me pull myself back into the mix of what's going on because I'm trying to escape." – *James*

Devise a plan, either a verbal plan or a symbolic plan, to say, "I want to recognize the fact that he or she's not here. I brought this candle along. I'd like to be able to light this candle in memory of my deceased loved one, and we'll just let that burn while we're here." – *Dr. Robert DeVries*

"I DON'T WANT TO BRING OTHERS DOWN"

"I didn't want to put a damper on anyone else's joy. So I put on a happy face and tried to be the sister, the daughter, the aunt, that everybody wanted to see. Putting on that happy face was a heavier burden than I was emotionally able to carry at the time," shares Mardie.

Pretending you are doing fine not only hurts you, but is unfair to those around you. "Other people have different expectations then," says Dr. Susan Zonnebelt-Smeenge. "They expect that you're doing well and that you won't need any more from them. You're sabotaging yourself if you aren't honest."

Think about times you've said, "I'm doing okay," when inside you were screaming the opposite. Being honest about your pain is a large part of moving forward through grief.

You have experienced a devastating loss. The fact that you are not feeling holiday cheer is normal. You are the one who needs to set the example for those around you that it's okay to talk about your lost loved one; it's okay to cry during a party or celebratory event; and it's okay to be sad when other people around you are happy.

"Therefore each of you must put off falsehood and speak truthfully to your neighbor, for we are all members of one body." (Ephesians 4:25)

Lord, I admit I've put on that happy-face mask. Help me to be honest with myself and with others so I can move forward and not backward in my grieving. Give me the humility to accept help, support, and prayers from others.

> REFLECT:
>
> Name the people you typically pretend around, saying "I'm okay" when you're not.
>
> What holds you back from being honest around those people?

TAKEAWAY:
It is okay to admit you are hurting, even when others think you shouldn't be.

SURVIVOR WISDOM

Advice and encouragement from people who know the pain of loss.

QUESTION: How Do You Respond to Comments and Questions at the Party?

You probably want to have a few things scripted beforehand that you're going to say to everybody when they ask. Then say those things very calmly: "This is where I am; this is what it is," and put a gracious end to the conversation [if desired]. If we don't have some things scripted beforehand, we can flounder, and that can makes us feel anxious and awkward. – *Omar King*

Other family members are looking to us, the grieving individual, for guidance [on how to treat you and how to honor your loved one] because they don't know what to do. So give them a little bit of guidance. – *H. Norman Wright*

Don't feel like you have to give explanations to people. If you want to respond to be polite, you can say something very general, "I'm going through the process," and then just change the subject. – *Zoricelis Davila*

When someone would say insensitive things, I would just speak words back to myself, "Sheila, you know they really don't understand. Give them grace. Forgive them. They don't know it's hurtful." – *Sheila*

What helps more than anything else is to be very honest when people ask how you are doing: "Thank you for asking; let me give you a summation. I'm struggling. I'm not always sure I'm going to be able to get through the entire day. I thought I was doing better this year, and some days I am, other days I'm not." Just be totally honest. That's healthy for you, but it's also healthy for the other individuals because in a way, you are teaching them about the journey of grief that they will have to go through at some time in their life. – *H. Norman Wright*

Every once in a while someone says something that's unhelpful, but who can relate to this? There's no right thing to say. I would rather walk through life with our friends and suffer an occasional unhelpful attempt than walk through this without them. So I'm grateful for their care. – *Carla*

SURVIVAL TIPS

The charts, checklists, and exercises in this section will help you apply the practical ideas in this book to your own life.

SOCIAL EVENT SURVIVAL

Preparation is key! These ideas can help make it easier for you to attend holiday and social events. Check the ideas that you might implement.

- ☐ Arrive late and/or leave early.

- ☐ Attend with someone who will run interference for you and help you interact with "well-meaning" people and who will understand when you're ready to leave. *Someone who could come with me:*
  _____

- ☐ Remember that during the holidays you might see people you haven't seen in a while. They might not be aware of the death and could ask after your loved one. *This is how I can respond:*
  _____

- ☐ Identify a place ahead of time where you can go for a while if you're emotionally overwhelmed. *Places I can retreat to in the home or building:*
  _____

- ☐ Sit in the back row or by the door, if applicable.

- ☐ Let the event host or your pastor know you will be there, so he or she can be aware of ways to help you.

- ☐ Beforehand, ask people to pray for you while you're at the event. *Someone I can ask:* _____

- ☐ Have someone you can call if you are attending the event alone and it becomes too much. *Someone I can call:*
  _____

WHAT TO SAY WHEN ...

You're invited to a party. You plan to attend, but have misgivings. People's questions and comments can be exhausting: *You just have to come. How are you doing? You're not yourself. Let go of your sadness for a little bit and just enjoy the party. Oh, I didn't mean to make you cry.*

Use these responses to help communicate with the host before you attend and with people at the party.

1. Send the responses to people in advance (you might combine more than one). Be sure to be gracious and appreciative of the invitation.
2. Write responses on an electronic device or paper for your own reference.

I Might Change My Mind Yes, I plan to attend. Please be aware I might change my mind or I might need to leave early. Do not feel bad or take it personally.	***Give Me Time to Respond*** Thanks for the invite. Is it okay if I take a few days to get back to you about this? If I forget to respond, please remind me. Because of the grief, I'm forgetting a lot of things these days.
Only for a Few Hours Thanks for the invite. I do plan to attend, but I'll only be able to stay for a few hours. If on that day I feel like staying longer, is it okay if I let you know then?	***I'm Not Ready*** Thank you for the invitation, but I'm not ready this year to spend several hours with others celebrating. Be sure to ask me again next year.
Don't Try to Cheer Me Up I know it might be difficult or uncomfortable to be around me right now. Please don't try to cheer me up or try to say something helpful. Please pray for me, and a hug and your presence is all I need.	***A Room to Excuse Myself To*** I might need to excuse myself to another room if I feel overwhelmed or need to be alone for a period of time. Please let me know in advance a room I could use.
Talking About My Loved One Please don't avoid talking about ___. Yes, I am sad and I might cry, but it's hurtful when people don't even mention his/her name.	***Don't Worry if I Cry*** Please be aware that I might start crying, and that's okay. Tears are part of my life right now and it's important that I allow myself to grieve.
Thank You for Praying and Caring I appreciate your prayers. Thank you for caring.	***Changing the Topic*** Thank you for asking. I'm working on that with God's help. But tell me what's new in your life [or, tell me how your parents/children/etc. are doing; tell me how your job is going].
Don't Set Me Up with Anyone I know you want what you think is best for me, but please don't try to set me up with anyone. It's important for me to focus on my healing and my spiritual and emotional health right now.	***Not Having Alcohol*** I'll just be having soda and water. While numbing my stress and pain is tempting, it's wiser for me to keep my head clear and make choices that are ultimately for my own good.
Plan a Visit for a Different Day I would love to spend time with you. Would it be okay if we plan a different time to get together when there won't be so many other people around? Are you available on [date/time]?	***Trying to Be Honest in My Grief*** Please understand I am trying to be honest in my grief. That means I will not be putting on a pretend face of holiday cheer. Despite my grief, I am thankful to be surrounded by people who care.

CONTROLLING NEGATIVE SELF-TALK WHEN YOU'RE ALONE

Spending time alone during the holidays can be productive, but a danger to avoid and prepare for is negative self-talk when you're alone. Here are some examples.

I can't do this. No one understands. If only I had ... It's all my fault. No one truly cares. I'm not going to make it. I'm not going to open myself to this kind of hurt again. There's nothing left to live for.

To control negative self-talk, you have to counter it with God's truth. Look at how Carla and Donna used Scripture to deal with the negative self-talk they were battling:

NEGATIVE SELF-TALK:

It's not true.

It does not build you up or help you grow.

It exaggerates the impact.

Negative self-talk: *"No one can relate to this. I'm really alone in this." – Carla*

If I feel alone this holiday, the truth is: God says He is with me, and He has given me people in my life who care for me. "The Lord is close to the brokenhearted" (Psalm 34:18a). "Finally, brothers and sisters ... encourage one another ... and the God of love and peace will be with you" (2 Corinthians 13:11). *"The truth is, God can equip other people to care for us." – Carla*

Negative self-talk: *"If I'd had my husband go do more tests, then maybe things would have turned out differently." – Donna*

If I am inappropriately blaming myself for the death, the truth is: God determined how long my loved one would live. "All the days ordained for me were written in your book before one of them came to be." (Psalm 139:16) *"There was nothing that I could have done that would have changed the outcome. That was my husband's time to go home." – Donna*

IN YOUR LIFE

What negative self-talk goes through your mind when you don't rein it in?

_____

Prayerfully write down a truth from God that you've learned.

_____

_____

TIPS FOR SURVIVING SOCIAL EVENTS GRIEFSHARE

HOLIDAY JOURNAL:

TIPS FOR SURVIVING SOCIAL EVENTS

Writing out thoughts and feelings, hurts and frustrations, helps you make sense of your feelings. Write your responses to one or more of the topics below in a separate notebook or journal. Or you could choose to write about a different topic.

- ☐ What concerns do you have about attending the different events and get-togethers coming up this season? (You could address each event separately.)
- ☐ How do you feel about attending church during the holidays?
- ☐ List the safe, uplifting people in your life you'll want to make a point to spend time with this holiday. Describe why you chose each of these people.
- ☐ Describe what has been the most difficult part of the holidays so far.

WHEN OTHERS DON'T UNDERSTAND, GRIEFSHARE IS THERE TO ENCOURAGE YOU

After the funeral, when the cards and letters have stopped coming, most people around you return to their normal lives. But your grief continues and you feel alone.

At a weekly GriefShare group, you'll find people who understand and who want to help as you rebuild your life.

Learn more at **www.griefshare.org**.

GRIEFSHARE

CHAPTER 4:

SURVIVING THANKSGIVING AND CHRISTMAS DAY

In normal years, Thanksgiving and Christmas days can be emotionally intense. This year, you may actually be dreading them, not sure if you can handle the activity, conversation, and the feelings you know will bubble to the surface. Be assured you can make it through. You'll also have the opportunity to honor and remember your loved one in tangible ways.

In this chapter you'll discover:

- How to focus on the true meaning of the holidays
- Ways to honor your loved one
- How to have peace amid the pain, whether or not it gets any easier

SURVIVOR STORIES

The first Christmas arrived, and Sabrina and Marion both attended family get-togethers.

"My sister-in-law was this great, fun-loving person, and I remember that first Christmas [after she had died] everybody still bought a gift for her. We bought fuzzy house shoes and stuffed animals, and we wrapped it all up, and when we brought the gifts to the house, they sat there. And we realized that she wasn't there to open them, and nobody wanted to open the gifts." – *Sabrina Black*

"The first Christmas that my husband passed, my daughter had just gotten married so we spent Christmas at her house, which was good, helping her during the hustle and bustle. But it was after everybody else had gone home, that was the difficult time. That was the time for my husband and me to simply watch a movie or clean up the leftovers or reflect on the day. It was saddest at the end of the day." – *Marion*

THE STRENGTH TO SURVIVE

These short daily readings will help you find a reason for hope in the face of sadness and despair.

CHERISH THE MEMORIES

Warm and happy memories of times spent with your loved one will always be part of your holiday seasons. Right now the memories may bring up deep pain, loneliness, floods of tears, regrets, and even anger. But over the years as you are healing, the memories will become precious and even bring tears of joy amid the sorrow.

"The memories are a gift. They're something I can look back on now and take pleasure in. It's a gift that I treasure," shares Mardie.

"My husband was a real character, and he kept us laughing," says Marion. "During the holiday celebrations [after his death], we would reflect on some of the things he would say. If somebody did something funny, we would say, 'This is probably what he would say or do in reaction to that.'

"It helps me to remember the good times, and there were good times. It's also very helpful when I talk about him and somebody listens to me; that's important to me."

Consider finding ways to preserve the memories. You could create a scrapbook, collage, quilt, shadow box, or photo album. Write about happy memories in a journal. Begin a new tradition over the holidays of each person sharing a memory of the deceased loved one, or sharing an important lesson learned from him or her. Don't hesitate to tell other people about special times with your loved one.

We can be thankful to God, for He always gives good gifts.

"For God so loved the world that he gave his one and only Son, that whoever believes in him shall not perish but have eternal life. For God did not send his Son into the world to condemn the world, but to save the world through him." (John 3:16–17)

God, I thank you for all the precious, happy memories with my loved one. My tears overflow when I think of how much love I have for this dear person. Thank you for blessing me with my loved one, and thank you for giving me an even greater blessing that lasts for eternity: the gift of life through Your Son Jesus.

REFLECT:
Brainstorm ideas of ways you could preserve and cherish special memories. Think of ideas suited to you.

TAKEAWAY:
Thank God for the cherished memories you have of your loved one.

HELP OTHERS WHO MIGHT NEED YOU

Consider spending Thanksgiving, Christmas, or New Year's with someone who is alone this holiday season: it could be someone who's experienced a death or a divorce, someone without family nearby, or a nursing home resident. If God puts the thought of a certain person on your heart, don't immediately dismiss that person because you don't think he or she would be interested. Take a chance. You might be pleasantly surprised.*

"After my mom passed, I [hosted Thanksgiving dinner] at my apartment. I also invited two students from the university, two young men from India. We were so busy trying to make these people feel at home that we didn't have time to wallow in our sadness," shares Lorraine.

You could also volunteer to help serve a holiday meal at a shelter, hospital, Salvation Army, fire or rescue station, or church. Find available opportunities in your community. Other ideas would be delivering cards or cookies to shut-ins or making encouraging phone calls.

"At the times I felt so low and so lonely," shares Mardie, "help came at just the right time, and if I can be that same gift to somebody else, what a blessing that is to me."

"Praise be to the God and Father of our Lord Jesus Christ, the Father of compassion and the God of all comfort, who comforts us in all our troubles, so that we can comfort those in any trouble with the comfort we ourselves receive from God. For just as we share abundantly in the sufferings of Christ, so also our comfort abounds through Christ." (2 Corinthians 1:3–5)

God, who needs my help and support? Who is hurting or alone or in need? Help me look at those around me with new eyes. Help me give Your comfort to someone else this holiday season. So many people are hurting, and many pretend everything is fine. Lead me to them. And give me the courage and energy to follow through.

TAKEAWAY:
Helping others eases your pain.

---

* *Always remember that inviting a person of the opposite sex is not wise if you've lost a spouse. A new relationship might be the last thing on your mind, but understand the other person might think differently. Your healing is of utmost importance, so do not jeopardize that.*

THE REASON FOR CELEBRATING THE HOLIDAYS

"It's important to remember that the holiday wasn't created simply for the relationship you had with your loved one, but that the holiday itself has a meaning that goes far deeper than any one relationship might have gone," explains Dr. Robert DeVries.

So what is the true meaning of Christmas?

"The true meaning of Christmas is about what God has done—that God has come near to us in Christ," says Dr. Alfonza Fullwood. "Christmas is about Christ. Christmas is a source of hope for those who are suffering because Christmas reminds me that God loves me. He's near me. He's come to me in His Son."

Consider what we are celebrating at Christmas:

Christ came to save us from our sin. He is with us always: "And she [Mary] will have a son, and you are to name him Jesus, for he will save his people from their sins … and they will call him Immanuel, which means 'God is with us.'" (Matthew 1:21–23 NLT)

God loves us so much. He sent His Son to save us from sin and give us eternal life: "For God so loved the world that he gave his one and only Son, that whoever believes in him shall not perish but have eternal life. For God did not send his Son into the world to condemn the world, but to save the world through him." (John 3:16–17)

Lord and Savior, You came to earth to save us and set us free from the worst darkness of all. Your birth is about hope, forgiveness, freedom, salvation, and most of all love. Help me to turn my focus to You, to consistently draw near to You, and to receive the gifts You are giving me.

TAKEAWAY:
Christmas is about Christ's coming to save the world from sin and suffering.

> REFLECT:
> Turn to pages xiii–xvi in this book. Prayerfully read the article "A Gift Beyond Comparison" and listen for what God is saying to you through His words and promises.

THE BASIS FOR HOPE

"When you've experienced a deep loss, it tends to dominate your life.

> You feel despair, but Jesus came to give you hope.
> You feel sadness, but Jesus came to bring joy into your life.
> Your life is in turmoil, yet Jesus came to bring peace to your life.
> Much of your time is dominated by tears, but Jesus came to wipe away every tear.

"He is your source of strength, and He is your stability." – H. Norman Wright

The Bible describes God's plan to remove suffering and provide us with lasting comfort and eternal life. To understand it, we need to see why we suffer in the first place. We suffer for many reasons: because we live in a world of sickness and disaster, because of the evil actions of others, and because of the consequences of our own disobedience to God (the Bible calls this "sin"). God is pure and holy: He cannot tolerate sin. Not only does our sin keep us from God, it also has consequences—suffering in this life and physical death followed by eternal punishment.

So, where is the hope? God loves us so much and does not want us to suffer. He has provided a way to release us from the penalty and presence of sin, both now and eternally. He sent His Son, Jesus Christ (who was sin-free), to be born on this earth and pay the penalty for our sins. Through Jesus, our sins are forgiven and our slate is wiped clean. And one day He will remove all sin and suffering from the world. This is reason for great hope.*

> REFLECT:
> What hope has God given you?
>
> This book has many Bible passages to encourage you and ground you in God's hope and truth. Set aside time to look them up in the Bible. A great time to read and reflect upon them is Christmas day.

"When God our Savior revealed his kindness and love, he saved us, not because of the righteous things we had done, but because of his mercy. He washed away our sins, giving us a new birth and new life … Because of his grace he declared us righteous and gave us confidence that we will inherit eternal life." (Titus 3:4–7 NLT)

Faithful God, I can trust You. You have a plan to take care of me, if I will turn my life over to You. Through You, we have the promise of everlasting life in an amazing place called heaven, a place that is just as real as the air I breathe.

TAKEAWAY:
God provides you with real hope amid your grief.

* To learn more, read the article "A Gift Beyond Comparison" on pages xiii–xvi.

DOES IT GET ANY EASIER?

Each holiday after your loved one's death will bring new changes, more memories, and new questions of "Will it be any easier this year?" Be encouraged that it does get easier.

"It may seem like you'll never get through dealing with this loss and pain, but with hard work and God walking alongside you, you will," encourages Dr. Susan Zonnebelt-Smeenge.

"When you get to the other side of that loss, you'll be able to remember the loss situation, and the positives and negatives associated with the person who's now lost. You'll be able to look afresh at what your life has at the present and the people who are around you. You'll be able to see your new purposes, and perhaps even the silver lining of how God uses pain to show us joy, and how sometimes going through difficulty will point us in directions we never would have believed were possible."

You will be able to laugh and enjoy the holidays again. You will be able to walk in thankfulness throughout each new year. With Jesus, darkness can never overcome you because He has defeated darkness, brokenness, and death (Revelation 21:4). And because of Christ, you can live with hope as you draw closer to Him and come to know Him intimately.

"I remember my affliction and my wandering, the bitterness and the gall … Yet this I call to mind and therefore I have hope: Because of the LORD's great love we are not consumed, for his compassions never fail. They are new every morning; great is your faithfulness." (Lamentations 3:19, 21–23)

Savior God, because of You, I have hope to keep me moving forward, one step at a time. I place my life in Your hands, knowing You are a sovereign God with a perfect plan—a plan that is much bigger than I can comprehend. I trust in You, realizing there is no one else to trust, no one like You. Forgive me for the times I've moved away from You or doubted You. Draw me into Your loving arms and empower me to walk forward in this life with You. Amen.

TAKEAWAY:
The pain of grief does lessen.

LOOKING BEYOND THE HOLIDAYS

"Finally, brothers and sisters ... encourage one another ... And the God of love and peace will be with you." (2 Corinthians 13:11)

The holidays are coming to an end, and the new year is approaching. As you continue to walk through the grieving process, you will need help and encouragement. The Bible says we were created to be in relationship with other people: to interact with, care for, encourage, and support. God wants us to accept help from other people.

"Healing from trauma or grief happens in the context of community. I don't know of any other way of finding healing that is not in the context of finding others who can help you," says David Bueno Martin.

> **REFLECT:**
> Who are the safe people in your life? Those who will not misjudge, but will listen to you, pray with you, cry with you, give you good counsel and point you to the Lord for help?

If you do not have people in your life who encourage you and point you toward God's help and healing, pray that God will lead you to safe, uplifting people who will walk alongside you on your grief journey.

"You have seen my troubles, and you care about the anguish of my soul. You have ... set me in a safe place." (Psalm 31:7b–8 NLT)

Lord, please guide me to people who will support and uplift me through my journey of grief. Give me the courage to take the step of reaching out to people for help. And thank you for the safety of Your presence and Your promises.

TAKEAWAY:
Make a point to be with people who will support and care for you through your grief process.

GriefShare is a safe place where others have an idea of what you are facing and want to help. To find a weekly GriefShare support group near you, go to **www.griefshare.org** or call **800-395-5755**.

SURVIVAL TIPS

The charts, checklists, and exercises in this section will help you apply the practical ideas in this book to your own life.

REMEMBERING AND HONORING YOUR LOVED ONE

To remember and honor your loved one this season, consider one of these ideas.

- ☐ Buy a small, live tree to plant in your yard. The tree will be there for years to come and can be decorated with lights each year.
- ☐ If you decide to hang stockings, include the missing family member's stocking. You or other family members can put a little gift or notes in the stocking.
- ☐ If your loved one had a particular heart or passion for children, animals, flowers, a certain cause, etc., volunteer an hour of your time or some money helping a local organization in his/her honor.
- ☐ Create a scrapbook, a photo collage, a quilt, a wood project, a garden, something in his/her honor.
- ☐ Find something simple, but meaningful, to place in your home to remember your loved one. A small vase with a single rose, a candle, a poinsettia plant, or a Christmas cactus (these can be planted outdoors).
- ☐ Buy or make an ornament that reminds you of your loved one.
- ☐ Visit the cemetery and decorate the grave with flowers, a small tree, or a cross.
- ☐ Sit around the dinner table or Christmas tree and talk about your loved one. Share good memories, lessons learned from your loved one, and character traits to exemplify.
- ☐ If your loved one had a favorite cookie/cake or meal, make that meal in his/her honor and give it to a person who would be thankful to receive it.
- ☐ Have a candle-lighting ceremony with your family or close friends. As each person lights a candle, he or she may share something meaningful about the loved one. People could also share a picture, song, poem, or a tangible item that was special to the loved one. End with a time of prayer.

☐ Have everyone share a special picture of your loved one and the memory associated with that picture.

☐ Plan a night of remembrance not only in honor of your lost loved one, but including other friends who have lost a loved one. Provide ornaments or have people bring a special ornament to hang on the tree in remembrance of their lost loved one. Invite people to share a special Christmas memory about their loved one. Include food, music, Scripture, and prayer.

YOUR LOVED ONE'S LEGACY

Part of a person's legacy is the good traits, lessons, deeds, and memories that he or she left with those still living. Your loved one's legacy lives on through you and through all the people your loved one touched in life. The holidays are a nice time to remember and record this legacy.

Write down valuable character traits that your loved one exemplified.
_____
_____

What good lessons have you learned from your loved one?
_____
_____

How will you make a point to pass on those good traits and lessons to other people?
_____
_____

IDEAS:

Send a note to family and friends asking them to write down a special memory and something they learned from your loved one. Compile them into a book to share.

At family get-togethers, plan to go around the room and share a humorous and happy memory of a time with your loved one. Or have everyone share your loved one's legacy in his/her life.

Start a memory journal. Fill your journal with special memories of times with your loved one. This journal will bring you much joy, laughter, and bittersweet tears in the years to come.

Be sure to tell others that it's okay for them to talk about your loved one in your presence.

BE THANKFUL

Thankfulness is a healing tool. There's always something to be thankful for:

"I'm grateful I had my father for as long as I did, that he was the person he was, and that God had uniquely given him to me." – Phil

"I'm so grateful Jesus made it possible for me to see my son again one day." – Hollis

"I am so grateful for our church and how well they've cared for us." – Carla

"I'm grateful that Christ came into my life. It's very hopeful to know I'm not alone." – Krista

"I'm grateful to have my family." – Shay

"I appreciate God's forgiveness because I know I can stand before God righteous. I thank God for the gift of my salvation." – Nicole

What are you thankful for?
Circle what you are thankful for.

>   The time I had with my loved one.
>
>   I'll see my loved one again.
>
>   My loved one is no longer suffering.
>
>   What I've learned from my loved one.
>
>   How God is helping me, comforting me, and providing for me in my grief.
>
>   My family.
>
>   My church.
>
>   My friends.
>
>   Good memories.
>
>   God and His promises.
>
>   My GriefShare group.

Write down anything else that you are thankful for today.

_____

_____

_____

_____

HELPING OTHERS HELPS YOU

A way to ease your loneliness and pain is to focus on helping others. There are so many opportunities for you to help others.

"One way you can shift your focus off of the pain is to focus on helping other people while you are hurting." – Dr. Alfonza Fullwood

"I called a lady in our church whose husband had died, and I left her a message. I knew exactly how her heart felt ... so empty. After she got home, she called me and said, 'You have no idea what your phone call meant.' When you reach out and help others, it helps your heart heal too." – Jeannine

Do not be overwhelmed by this list. Carefully read the ideas, and mark any that might suit you. These ideas are just to help you broaden your thinking of areas where you could help. If you are not ready for this right now, that's completely fine.

Call, invite over, visit, or send a card/gift

- ☐ Elderly friend/homebound person
- ☐ Someone with no family in the area
- ☐ Exchange student/international university student
- ☐ Single-parent family or a single parent alone this holiday
- ☐ Someone grieving a loved one's death
- ☐ Someone facing a separation or divorce or marital problems
- ☐ A family or child in financial need
- ☐ Someone who has comforted you
- ☐ Other idea: _____

Help a family, friend, or group with a physical/practical need

- ☐ Staying with an ill loved one to provide a break for the caregiver
- ☐ Child care, especially for a single parent
- ☐ Gardening/yard work
- ☐ Painting/repairs
- ☐ Housework
- ☐ Meals
- ☐ Other idea, suited to your skills/strengths: _____

Serve others in need through a local organization
- ☐ Nursing home/assisted living facility
- ☐ Soup kitchen
- ☐ Salvation Army
- ☐ Women's shelter/pregnancy center
- ☐ Jail/prison
- ☐ Detention home
- ☐ Volunteering at a walk/run for a cause
- ☐ Church ministries
- ☐ Library/community organizations
- ☐ Rescue squad

Pray that God will bring to mind someone who needs your words, your hands, your prayers this season. Your church pastor will also have suggestions of people who are alone this holiday season and places to volunteer.

Make a list of people and their needs, and pray for them

- ☐ _____
- ☐ _____
- ☐ _____

"Serve one another humbly in love" (Galatians 5:13b)

HOLIDAY JOURNAL:
SURVIVING THANKSGIVING AND CHRISTMAS DAY

Use a separate notebook or journal to write out your responses to one or more of the topics below. Remember that your journal is for you; what you record is between you and God.

- ☐ Describe your favorite Christmas memories of your loved one.

- ☐ Name some of your favorite gifts that you received from your loved one. What was the first gift you remember receiving from your loved one?

- ☐ Write a response to God in light of the fact that He is with us. Share your thoughts honestly with God, and take time to listen for what He wants to say to you.

  "One of the main messages of Christmas is that God not only exists, but He leans in, He cares, and He's involved. Our God is not a distant, detached observer, but God in Christ Jesus, Immanuel, is with us, and He is for us. We're not alone." – Dr. Ramon Presson

- ☐ Christ is coming again to join with Him all who've given their hearts to Him—both those in heaven and on earth. Express in your journal what you are thankful for regarding Christ's coming.

TAKE INVENTORY

When the holiday season comes to a close this year, we encourage you to take inventory of these past several weeks.

What ideas did you implement that worked well?

_____

_____

_____

What didn't work or was stressful?

_____

_____

_____

What do you think you'll do differently next year?

_____

_____

_____

List the three most important ideas you've learned from the Surviving the Holidays program.

_____

_____

_____

IF YOU FEEL SUICIDAL

Thoughts of wanting to escape the pain are normal in grief, and you may even have thought you cannot live without your loved one. If you have considered taking your life or how you would plan to do that—pick up the phone.

"Many times individuals have thoughts of, I just don't want to live anymore," says H. Norman Wright, an expert in crisis counseling and intervention. *"Anytime you have a pattern of suicidal thinking, let somebody else know, because the main problem right now is that the only person you're talking with is yourself, and you're not getting good advice from yourself.* Find somebody you trust. It could be a pastor, a counselor, a very good friend who is going to listen to you.

"Realize that fleeting thoughts like this are quite normal, but when it becomes a pattern, then it becomes more serious. Never neglect it; never ignore it. Reach out. It might be one of the most difficult things you have to do, but reach out and let somebody else assist you, walk with you, and loan you his or her faith and hope at this time when yours is so low. That way you'll be able to get through it."

What to do if you feel suicidal:

1. Call 911 or go to the emergency room.
2. Call a friend, family member, doctor, pastor, or counselor immediately, and tell that person you're feeling suicidal. You should not be alone.
3. Call a suicide help line, such as 1-800-273-TALK (8255). Keep these phone numbers by your telephone or saved in your cell phone.

The Bible includes many records of men and women crying to God in desperation and honesty. You can follow their example by reading their words as your prayer to God. A great example can be found in Psalm 61. Read these verses when you have time. For now, here's a prayer that you can cry out to God.

God, I'm overwhelmed. I don't like thinking or feeling the way I am right now, and I want all this to stop. Help me remember that You see my tears and hear my every thought. I am frozen and don't know what to do or who to turn to. Help me to trust that You are with me, even now, and to trust there is no problem or situation too big for You to handle. Guide and direct me to the person or the help I need. Thank you for loving me, and thank you for the Bible because it points me to hope. In Jesus' name, Amen.

GRIEFSHARE RESOURCES

GriefShare support groups
Attend a weekly GriefShare support group, where you can share your emotions in a safe place and learn helpful insights on how to walk the journey of grief. To find a list of groups near you, go to **griefshare.org**.

Surviving the Holidays website
At **griefshare.org/holidays** find articles, real-life stories, and video clips to help you reduce stress, minimize loneliness, and discover a healthy approach to the holiday season after the death of a loved one.

A Season of Grief free daily email messages
Receive an encouraging email message every day for a year. Sign up for these free messages at **griefshare.org/dailyemails**. You can also email a friend who is hurting and encourage him or her to sign up. (The messages are an online version of the book *Through a Season of Grief*.)

Grieving with Hope
This powerful, GriefShare-based book contains short, topical chapters addressing issues that grieving people face but are often hesitant to mention to others; it helps people accurately interpret the message their emotions are sending them and gently guides them to determine whether they're grieving in a way that leads to hope and ultimate healing. Look for *Grieving with Hope* by Samuel Hodges and Kathy Leonard at a local or online bookstore or at **griefshare.org/hope**.

Through a Season of Grief devotional
This book of 365 short, daily messages is based on the GriefShare program. Each day you will be equipped with biblical comfort and practical teaching to help you take steps forward toward healing. Look for *Through a Season of Grief* by Bill Dunn and Kathy Leonard at a local or online bookstore or at **griefshare.org/devotional**.

Tell a friend about GriefShare
If you know someone hurting because of loss, make sure he or she knows about GriefShare by using the share tools at **griefshare.org**. You can share a GriefShare page via email or your social networks.

How to help grieving children
If you have school-age children dealing with grief, the "How to Help Grieving Children" video offers suggestions and helps answer tough questions you might have in caring for them. View this video at **griefshare.org/children**.

Other online help
At **griefshare.org**, print and use the "Help for the Journey" personal Bible study, read the "God, What Is Going On?" pages, and learn more about the GriefShare program. Find helpful videos at the GriefShare YouTube channel, **youtube.com/griefshare**. Visit our Facebook page at **facebook.com/griefshare**.

WEEKLY ENCOURAGEMENT AS YOU REBUILD YOUR LIFE

GriefShare is a friendly, caring group of people who will walk alongside you through one of life's most difficult experiences. You don't have to go through the grieving process alone.

Learn more at **www.griefshare.org**.

GRIEFSHARE